Out of the Darkness

My Journey through Foster Care

Kailamai Hansen

Out of the Darkness: My Journey through Foster Care
Copyright © 2015 by Kailamai Hansen

All rights reserved. No part of this book may be reproduced or transmitted in any form or by any means without written permission from the author. Certain names and locations may have been changed for privacy reasons.

Cover Photo: Brittany Amburn
Editors: Carrie May Anderson & Sasha Hoffman

Printed in USA by 48HrBooks (www.48HrBooks.com)

Dedication

To all who believed in me. Richard Paul Evans, you are a blessing beyond words. You make me want to be a better person. Thank you for inspiring me to write again. Jenna, for walking me through this process and for loving me along the way.

To my parents, Mai-Ting, Casey, Stan and Loren, Bev & Sky. Mai-Ting, my mother, I love and miss you. I hope you are proud of your Bug. Casey, my consistent, sparkling rock. Stan, you encouraged me to reach for the stars, I couldn't have done it without you. Loren, you make your babygirl smile. Bev, you are my sound mind when I am lost. I love you dearly. Sky, thanks for always checking in and leaving me sweet voicemails. Hoang Chau (my Chris), how did I get so blessed? Peanut, you will always be my sister and best friend. Malia, the big sister I never had. Josalun, your laughter will make me live longer. Chuck and Linda, your love amazes me. My nieces and nephews; you make my heart sing. Lynn, Martha, and Leslie, the teachers who made learning my safe place.

Falen, Janet, Todd, Wendy and Michelle for all you invest in Idaho's youth. Tiffany, one day at a time. Misty. Most importantly, my Heavenly Father, whom I am nothing without. Whom, by his grace, I have lived to tell my story.

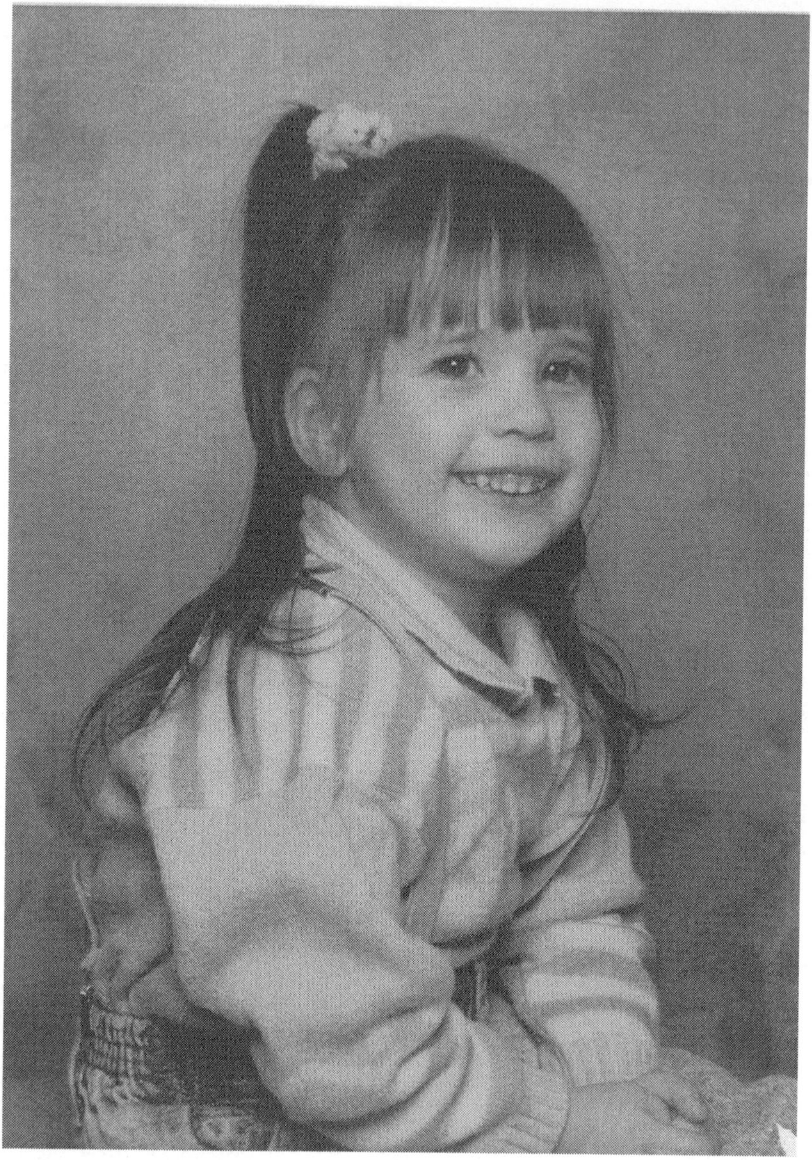

Table of Contents

Dedication	3
Preface	6
Chapter 1	7
Chapter 2	19
Chapter 3	25
Chapter 4	30
Chapter 5	35
Chapter 6	41
Chapter 7	48
Chapter 8	57
Chapter 9	61

Preface

It wasn't until a foggy morning in February 2001 that everything changed. I was in the counselor's office of my middle school, and for the first time, someone was asking me to tell them the truth.

I took a hasty breath in, a tear making its way down my cheek. My knees knocked as fear rushed through me.

"Now dear, tell me what happened." The gentle, petite counselor leaned forward, peering into my eyes. I could sense her concern, but still I hesitated.

Silence.

"How's your life at home?" she questioned.

Silence.

"You can trust me."

In that instant, I mustered up the courage to look up at her. Something about her sincerity soothed me. I sensed something unfamiliar: trust. The floodgates holding my pain were bursting at the seams, and I could no longer hold ground.

It was then that I told my story for the first time, and my life was never to be the same.

Chapter One

My early childhood memories are a cluster of different experiences and fibers of scattered memories. Sometimes I wake in the dead of the night and recall a memory for the first time. Tears, anger and sorrow visit me until I am too tired to process it and I retire for the night. Other memories I spend sleepless nights trying to erase, wishing I hadn't seen the chaos unfold, or that I didn't hear those two words: "She's dead." This is my story, to the best of my knowledge, how I recall it.

In my earliest memory I remember living in a blue house out in the mountains. My sister and I would play trolls and roam the land with the neighbor girl. The trees smelt of pine and our home was a city of its own. We would watch for falling stars when the sky was clear and the stars sparkled with all their might. We wished upon those stars and had dreams we yearned to fulfill. We were kids just like any other.

Growing up my mother wasn't around much. She grew up in the low income division of a small logging town in northern Idaho. She became pregnant with my sister Amanda in her senior year of high school, and subsequently dropped out.

I never met my father. There is speculation as to who he is, but my mother hardly mentioned him, so neither did I. My mom had a few boyfriends here and there. All stayed a few years, but none of them committed. They ended up leaving for some reason or another. Each had their own set of problems. One was an alcoholic, another a drug addict, most of them violent. The worst one was the pervert. At a young age I recall walking from a bedroom to the living room in an unfamiliar house. I carried a white plastic laundry basket, the bottom filled with my belongings. I dragged it behind me as I hiked up the slanted floor, not looking up. He was drinking at the table with a few other guys playing cards. It's a bit foggy for me now but I vividly remember his hands down my pants, and his liquor-saturated breath panting, "Be quiet." I was too scared to tell, wondering if anyone would believe me. Shame kept me quiet and the incident became one of my many secrets.

My mom felt trapped in the small town, and created a prison for herself with the lifestyle she adopted to escape her problems. She was raised by her stepfather and birth mother who had moved from Seattle shortly after her birth. She told me stories growing up about how she had been abused. The abuse was so severe that she was placed on disability for PTSD from the trauma. It was a time when what happened in the home, stayed in the home. It is heart-wrenching that no one stepped in to help and remove her. As a result, she parented the only way she knew how. Abuse, anger, and chaos were familiar to her, and so the cycle continued.

Prior to the age of five I only have a few memories. The smell of paint and apple juice brings me back to the blue house. The feel of grass and the taste of dirt place me in the metal-fenced front yard. I don't have many memories of my mother other than her scent, touch, and absence. I know I missed her. I know I looked for her when she was gone and waited with my breath held until she returned. I remember missing her.

Shortly after turning five, our lives began to radically change. My mother joined a dart league and was gone more often. In her first year on the league, she met and started dating a man named Andy. On the league together, they would stay at the bar drinking until it closed, then come home and get high. This was when meth was first introduced into my family, at least in front of me. This was when I started to lose my mother. She became addicted to meth. The league consumed her time, and the addiction consumed her soul.

She quickly became unaware of the life that surrounded her. Andy turned abusive as soon as he got comfortable, and not too long after a mining accident nearly killed him and impaired his ability to act rationally. Physical violence quickly crept into our home and became a new means of functioning.

My mother suffered abuse from Andy almost daily. Words cut her soul as he demeaned her as a human being. The accident changed him and caused his temper to easily flare. In the blink of an eye he would turn from content to angry and lash out at my mom. Though abuse was familiar, it was still unwelcome.

Over time she became angry. She began to take her frustrations out on my sister and me. It started at first with an aggressive shake or a forceful shove. As I got older she turned to slapping me and pulling my hair.

In her fits of rage she would drag me by my hair, yelling about different, irrelevant topics. She would get angry and leave for days. Even though she was violent, I still missed her. I needed her. Did she know what she was doing to me, how my heart was breaking without her there to comfort me? I knew her heart. It was compiled of gold, but robbed at an early age by violence.

Around age six, we moved from our blue home to a studio apartment above the bar where my mom played darts. The three of us lived in the studio, and Andy lived down the hall. Many nights I would sit in the bar and watch my mom play. I would order jumbo fries and stick my straw through them out of boredom. I would stack all of my fries on the straw like a skewer, then eat them one by one. When sleepy, I would leave and go up to the studio to fall asleep.

My sister and I were home together alone most days. Our studio window opened to the roof overlooking the street below, and at night we would climb out the window and throw eggs over the roof at the drunk people leaving the bar. Sometimes we would sleep on the roof and look for our falling stars.

As a child I improvised on my playtime. I would roam the town, searching for warmth and happiness. I would watch families sitting around their dinner tables enjoying a hot meal, imagining myself loved like that one day. I would go sledding at the local park, wearing three pairs of socks around my thin mittens to keep warm. During the summer I loved to hunt salamanders at the pond nearby. On the weekends I would bike to our city pool and play in the water till my fingers rippled like prunes. Watching the families around me at the park distracted me from my life at home.

At the age of seven my mom, sister, Andy and I moved to what I call the "peach house". Once we moved in, a kind neighbor lady named Kay started talking to my sister and I over the fence as she watered her garden. She invited us over to help us with our homework, and enjoyed reading us stories. She had a shaggy dog named Gus, and I would sometimes pretend I was reading to him. Kay's eyes sparkled as I discovered new books, my smile growing with each new page. She got excited each time I made new progress. She taught me to love reading.

Kay used to come over to check on my sister and me since my mom was gone often. In the mornings she would come over to wake us up and feed us breakfast before sending us to school. One time she came over and we did not have electricity because my mom failed to pay the bill. Kay called child protective services, and they came to investigate.

Child protective services removed my sister and me and placed us in a foster home. I vaguely remember the move, but have no recollection of the stay. We were placed in care for a short period of time, then the state moved us back home with our mom. My mom had agreed to pay the electricity and seek financial assistance to better care for my sister and me.

Andy and my mom continued down their path of destruction, and Andy became more violent and enraged. In one altercation, Andy pinned my mom down on the bed and was choking her. He spit in her face as he held her down and yelled at her. Afraid, I ran and hid in the hall closet. My sister Amanda was now ten and knew to call the police. She grabbed the phone off the wall and ran for the stairs. She called 911 and hid mid-flight. Her words were muffled as she cried to the operator, fearful of what was coming next. Andy heard her on the phone and charged to where she was on the stairs. Ripping the phone out of her hand he dragged her to the bathroom where he pushed her across the floor. He grabbed her by the back of the neck and put her head in the toilet. He slammed the lid down multiple times on her neck as she cried for him to stop. Amanda's screams and the cries of my mom bled together as I hid and quietly cried, waiting.

It seemed like an eternity by the time the police arrived. Once inside, they located Andy and pulled him off. I got the courage to look out the door just in time to see them tackle and arrest him.

Amanda and I were then sent to our second foster home. I vaguely remember the second home, although my sister said it was with a single woman who had land up the river. She said we would play down by the water during the day, and in the yard at night making forts. I do remember, however, swallowing a quarter and watching the T.V. show MASH.

After six months we were sent home. Andy was still living with us, and not much had changed. My sister got a pet pigeon and named it Linny. Growing up, he was our only pet (other than a hermit crab I won at the fair). Linny lived in a cupboard in Amanda's room and we would take him out often to play house.

Amanda and I built safe places around the house to hide during the fights. We had a long hallway that connected our rooms and many nights I would find my way over to her. I mainly hid, younger and terrified, whereas Amanda tried to protect our mom.

One Thanksgiving a fight erupted over what meat was to be bought for dinner. My mom insisted on ham whereas Andy wanted turkey. The fight escalated quickly and turned violent in a matter of moments. Knowing what was next, I hid in the hall closet as my sister screamed at Andy to stop hitting our mom. I could hear plates breaking and things hitting the floor. I covered my ears and closed my eyes.

Andy ended up stabbing my mom in the thigh with a fork. He also shoved my sister and hit her as she tried to intervene. Police arrived shortly after and took him to jail. Andy was our main source of financial support as my mom was on disability. Since he was in jail, we could no longer afford our home and had to move.

The next house we lived in only had two bedrooms. My mom lived in the main bedroom, and my sister the other. My room was the enclosed front porch. During cold months, I would come in the house at night freezing and afraid. There was no heat in my room, and the cold was unbearable. To keep my mind distracted from the disorder at home I would resort to books. As a nine year old, this was the best way I could come up with to cope.

Andy returned home from jail a few months later. One evening, my sister walked into the house while he was weighing out the drugs he had just purchased. Angry that she walked in on him, he rose to his feet. She spoke cautiously as she attempted to explain that she only had come inside to get a shovel. She assured him she would leave right after she got it. As she walked past him he reached out and grabbed her by the arm. He overpowered her and used his strength to shove her hard. Her body flew over the couch and she landed headfirst on the floor. Her neck was bent between the couch and coffee table. First tears streamed from her face, then anger fueled her to fight back. She was tired of Andy hurting her and in that moment had the courage to try and stop him. She started to yell at him when he picked her up off the floor. He yelled at her to go to her room and as she resisted he shoved her toward her bedroom. Cursing and shouting, they fought back and forth. She pulled her arms from his grip and smacked him away, which only made him more angry. He then thrust her head against the nearby water heater. Satisfied, he turned and left as she lie still, eyes closed. She had blacked out.

Amanda survived the incident, but emotionally, she may as well have been dead. Andy was again sent to jail, my sister was placed in another home, and I stayed with my mom.

The state condemned the house we lived in because it had traces of lead and forced us to leave. We moved to an apartment complex three blocks away from our old house. It took us two days to move our belongings from one place to the other. Unable to afford a moving truck, we piled our stuff into shopping carts from the local grocery store.

My mom finally left Andy, and my sister was returned home. Amanda did her best to shield me from danger, but she was a child herself. Her childhood was filled with protecting me, as she watched over me when my mom was gone. She recently told me a story about when we were younger that illustrates just how long she had been caring for me. I was crying in my crib, and she thought that I was hungry. Being three years older than me, she didn't know how to cook. After rummaging through the cupboards, she came across a cylinder of dried oats. She opened the lid and poured the oats into my crib. It must have distracted me, because I stopped crying. Her logic was funny, but her situation was not. She was robbed of her childhood, due to mothering me.

She started to get closer with school friends and relied on those friendships to help her stay distracted and busy. I, on the other hand, leaned toward school, especially reading. School was an interesting place for me. I loved it because for seven hours a day, I could escape home and pretend life was different. During lunch I would go to the library to find new books to read. *Goosebumps* books were my favorite. I'd rent a few books at a time and take them home with me. My mom did the best she could, but our home was filthy and unsafe. Some nights I slept on piles of laundry or the floor. Whatever environment I was in, books were my escape. I would cling to them as I walked home, curious as to where they would take me that night. I dreamt of things I read in the books such as saving people and making the world a better place. As soon as I got home I would sneak to the laundry room and set up shop. Snacks in hand, I would pull out all my books and choose which to read first. Once comfortable, I began my journey through the text, and page by page I temporarily escaped my life.

I invested my free time into doing homework and maintained decent grades. School was promising and I smiled at the thought of my education turning me into the woman I hoped to become. I knew it could take me places. In that aspect I loved school, but on the other hand, I dreaded it. I was bullied at school for being overweight and a tomboy. I had no sense of style and wore my sister's hand-me-downs or clothes my mom stole from the Goodwill dumpster. I was bullied for who my mother was known as around town. I was bullied for being dirty and constantly being sent home for having lice. Full of shame, I would stagger home crying out of fear and embarrassment, knowing that my hair would have to be cut off again. I was bullied for who I was.

Despite the obstacles with other kids, I still considered school to be my best refuge, and by fifth grade the school library was my favorite place to be. As things at home got worse, I focused harder on my studies. Every day after school I would work on projects in the school cafeteria until the janitor told me I had to go home. I found joy in learning.

As I relied more on school for belonging, my sister Amanda started experimenting with drugs. Part of that was due to my mother's new boyfriend, Jeff. Jeff had lived across the street from us, and would spend the whole day sitting on his stoop, observing. Cigarette in hand, he sat back and watched as life unfolded in front of him. He rarely spoke to me, just watched me play. He creeped me out and after only a few interactions with him I felt uneasy by his presence.

Jeff was stern in his discipline with me, and he made it known that he was in charge of the house. My mother fell into her submissive role as she did with Andy, and Jeff took over. Jeff, my mom, and Amanda would smoke marijuana and drink in the living room while they played Rummy. They would eat potato chips and blare AC/DC as they passed the joint around. I was eleven and Amanda was fourteen. At this young age she started to fall deep into terrible habits just like our mom. The last few years of extreme abuse left Amanda angry and broken. With no one to lean on, she relied on drugs and alcohol for temporary numbness. It was the one way she could truly be distracted from the pain. Jeff and Amanda would smoke together and bonded through drugs. Amanda would stay away from home as long as possible, then return late at night, knocking things over as she stumbled through the hallway. When things didn't go her way she started resorting to violence, and it became her way of coping. Jeff urged her to discipline me and she did in the only way she knew how. It began with her punching my arm when I would say something she disliked. As with my mother and Andy, it escalated quickly. Punches turned into kicks, and kicks to hair pulling and shoving. One night I complained about being woken up on a school night and she returned my complaint with a few quick blows to my chest and neck, followed by a kick as she walked by my crouched-up body on the floor. She came out of nowhere, her anger unwarranted. Amanda got used to getting her way with violence and it became almost a daily ritual. She slowly hardened as the drugs and alcohol ate away at her. Hurt and confused, she needed a way to let go of the anger she harbored due to the abuse, and the lack of a childhood. Somehow, Jeff saw joy in this. During a fight he would egg her on. When I cried for help he would snicker, "You've got to fight your own battles," as if offering me wise counsel. I became weak and helpless as I realized I was the black sheep in the family. Strong in my morals, I didn't believe in violence. As Dr. Martin Luther King said, "Returning violence for violence multiplies violence, adding deeper darkness to a night already devoid of stars". I knew violence was not the answer, even though it was all I had been taught. When Amanda fought me, I braced myself and took what I could. I reminded myself of how I had gotten through every other fight, and this one was no different. I rationalized that Amanda didn't mean to hurt me. My mom never tried to stop Amanda, but she seemed to pity me later; I wasn't sure if the glisten in her eyes were tears of sorrow for her child, or for her inability to help.

By the end of my fifth grade school year Amanda and I had virtually stopped talking. I felt alone and abandoned as my one confidant left me home alone to fend for myself. She started dating and had her boyfriend over when she was home. Whenever my mom told her do something, Amanda would mouth off and it would start a fight. I usually hid in my bedroom, watching the chaos through a hole in the wall.

One fight was particularly frightening to me. My mom was yelling at Amanda for terrorizing the house when she was home. She was loud and bossy and my mom was at her wit's end. My mom was sitting in the recliner chair eating her dinner as the fight broke out. They yelled back and forth and my sister refused to give in. As the fight got worse my mom went to move out of her chair. In anger, my sister stomped on the foot of the recliner, trapping my mom's feet in the fold. The plate of hot food in her hand flipped over, spilling steaming corn and potatoes on her lap. Frightened and stuck, my mom started crying. With just moments to think, I ran to the living room. I approached her chair and tried to help her up. My sister's anger shifted toward me as I told her to stop and that she had gone too far.

I don't recall what happened between that moment and the moment I woke up face down on the kitchen floor. I woke to Amanda straddling my hips and pounding into my lower back with her fists. I cried out for her to stop, and the room started spinning. Pain radiated from my lower back up my spine and into my shoulders. I wondered when she would stop and started hyperventilating as the fear inside me grew. I attempted to pull away and rather exhausted myself in the process. The sound of my crying softened as I slowly gave in and stopped fighting back. She finally finished with me and stood. I crawled to the bathroom cautiously as I was scared she would change her mind and start over. I reached the bathroom and grabbed onto the base of the toilet. I pulled myself up over the seat and started puking. Chunks of blood filled the toilet and I began choking on my tears. I gagged and vomited until I was too weak to hold myself up. When the puking subsided, I closed my eyes and slipped away from the madness, feeling nothing but appreciation for silence.

I woke in the hospital a few hours later. I had machines beeping and pumping around me. Bright lights filled the room and I clenched my eyes shut. A needle rested in my left arm, and there was a nurse by my side. When I came to I kept quiet, hoping it was a dream.

That was the day my mom decided it was time to move again, this time out of the city. The state had threatened to take me and my sister away if we didn't relocate to a place where my family could get the help they needed. My mom decided to move to Coeur d' Alene. It was a beautiful town about an hour away from where we lived. On the first of the month we would go over the hill to Coeur d' Alene to do our grocery shopping. I knew the town was much bigger and it had more schools for my sister and me. There were better treatment and parenting classes for my mom as well. I looked forward to a fresh start in a new city and smiled at the thought of not knowing anybody. This new city held many promises of positive change, but I didn't hold my breath.

Chapter Two

Shortly after we moved to Coeur d'Alene, Jeff and my mom got married. I can still see my mom's smile as she waited anxiously at the altar. Her long brown hair was down and wavy, with white flowers pinned in her hair. This was the only time I ever saw my mother in a dress, and she was beautiful.

Our new home in Coeur d'Alene was a three bedroom apartment. We lived six blocks from my new middle school, so I walked to school each morning. As I had before, I quickly found and loved the library. I worried about being bullied but had developed my self-identity and wanted to make friends. I started to introduce myself and speak up in class. Making friends came naturally and I soon felt I had plenty. I was still bullied for my weight but not as often. I became close with my friend Morgan and would share my hopes and dreams with her. She asked questions about my life and family but I didn't have much to say. Abuse was still constant at home, and Morgan began to notice scratches and bruises on my arms and neck. One day she asked me what had happened to me but I didn't want to tell her. Although she was young, she knew that something was wrong. She decided to try to help me.

Our school counselor's name was Deborah, and she kept a large white board outside of her office for students to sign their names on when they needed to talk to her. Morgan walked me down to the office and wrote my name on the board. Later that day I was called down to the office.

Once in Deborah's office, the fear of my situation sunk in. I felt like I was in trouble. I was unsure of what to do, so I sat quietly and listened. She explained to me that she was there to listen and that I was in a safe place to share whatever I needed to talk about. She started listing situations of abuse and then questioned me. My cheeks flushed as I recalled the fight I had with my mom that morning. She had yelled at me, though I am unsure now of why. As part of my punishment, I was not allowed to shower and was sent to school dirty and ashamed. Feelings of abandonment and neglect rushed over my heart, and my emotions got the best of me. I became upset as I let my guard down a little. Someone wanted to talk to me. Me. Someone wanted to listen to what I had to say. I took a hasty breath in, a tear making its way down my cheek. My knees knocked as fear rushed through me.

"Now dear, tell me what happened." The gentle, petite counselor leaned forward, peering into my eyes. I could sense her concern, but still I hesitated.

Silence.

"How's your life at home?" she questioned.

Silence.

"You can trust me."

In that instant, I mustered up the courage to look up at her. Something about her sincerity soothed me. I sensed something unfamiliar: trust. The floodgates holding my pain were bursting at the seams, and I could no longer hold ground.

We talked, and as I told her about my life at home I felt a tremendous weight being lifted off my shoulders. I felt relieved to tell someone, and feel like they genuinely cared. She listened intently, and as I described instances, I saw her face turn pale and grimace. She grieved for me as I peeled the layers back one by one. When I was finished, Deborah excused herself to make a few phone calls. While she was away I attempted to process what had just happened. Thoughts raced through my mind and confusion set in.

About ten minutes later Deborah returned with an apple and some fruit snacks.

"Okay, here's the plan," she told me. "Tonight when you get home, quietly go to your room. Pack a few night clothes and the basics. Do not tell anyone what is going on, just keep to yourself. Someone will come for you around 5 o'clock. Okay?"

"Okay," was all I could muster.

I was confused and scared at the same time. Had I done the right thing? Who did she call?

Deborah could tell I was upset and she reached for my hands. Gently she placed them in hers, and her eyes became misty. She looked at me with sorrow and promised that everything would be okay.

Somehow, I believed her.

As I walked home from school, questions filled my mind. Who was coming for me? Where would they take me? Would I be in trouble for telling? Mom will be so mad. What have I done?

As I approached the front door, I grasped the gold knob, twisting it slowly before venturing inside. I set down my book bag and slipped off my shoes. Mom and Jeff were watching T.V., and Amanda was cooking Top Ramen in the kitchen. I went quietly to my room, unnoticed as usual. I found a duffel bag in my closet and started packing. Three days' worth of clothes and a portable CD player fit perfectly inside. I rummaged for my journal and tucked it in the side zipper with a metallic blue pen. Then I waited. I sat in the middle of my room on the floor with my legs crossed, waiting for someone to come.

Just then, Amanda barged into my room demanding I tell her where her black pants were. I insisted I didn't know, but she didn't believe me. She started throwing my things around, searching for her pants. Her anger was building and I knew this was not going to end well. I braced myself.

"I don't have your stupid pants!" I bawled, suddenly emotional. "Leave me alone!"

She lowered her head to become eye level with me and hissed, "You've always wanted to be me, fat ass, now tell me where they are!"

I insisted I didn't have her pants and pleaded with her to leave, but she wouldn't budge. As she tore through my room she shoved me by my shoulders, knocking me on my back. I reached for her foot and tripped her, which only fueled her anger. She snatched me by my hair and dragged me kicking and screaming out of the room towards the stairs. I grasped for the carpet and any object I could reach. I kicked my feet and screamed as the carpet tore at my bare skin. Once at the top she shoved me down and my body fell forward. Reaching out my hands I grabbed for the railing and caught myself halfway down. Bravery filled my body, and I snapped. Frustrated and tired of the abuse, I charged her. Years of rage consumed me and propelled me up the stairs to where she was standing. We lunged at each other and fought with a deep-rooted hate. We hit and scratched each other as each of us attempted to overpower the other. I took all the built up anger I had for her and pushed my body hard into hers, sending her down the stairs. She tumbled to the bottom and immediately looked at me as she landed. Afraid, I froze. Surprise filled her eyes as she looked at me in disbelief. I stood up for myself for the first time. I was no longer a little girl.

No words were exchanged as I left the stairway and headed to the bathroom. My mom had been sitting on the couch the whole time. As I passed her she didn't even look up, and my pain turned back into anger. I cursed at her for letting my sister hurt me. Even though I could see the sadness in her eyes, she didn't move.

"They're taking me anyways," I shot at her.

"Who?" was Jeff's response, "Who would want you?"

"They're coming for me, just wait," I said.

My heart became heavy as I turned back to the stairs. I slowly walked up to my room, hoping it was close to five. I got my duffel bag out of my bedroom, wrapped its long strap around my wrist, and dragged it behind me on the floor. I rested six steps from the bottom of the stairs and waited. I could hear voices talking below me, but my head was pounding and my heart was aching. I didn't attempt to make out what they were saying, but rather gave in to the fatigue and closed my eyes.

A loud knock on the door jolted me awake. A deep man's voice pounded through the door. "Coeur d' Alene Police, open up!"

What? The police? Deborah sent the police? I leaned over the side of the stairs to see what was happening. Six policemen and one lady made their way into the living room. The lady saw me, and made her way through the men. I remember a lot of yelling and confusion as she motioned for me to follow her outside. I wasn't sure what to feel and tears filled my eyes and toppled over onto my cheeks. She walked over to me and picked up my bag, then held my hand and led me towards the door. I looked for my mom and found her handcuffed on the couch.

"I'm sorry, I love you, mom," I pleaded. Sorrow and guilt panged my heart as I saw her confined that way. She looked down at the floor and ignored me. She remained silent. This was my fault, I caused this. That was one of the worst feelings I have ever experienced—feeling like the person who should love you the most may not love you at all.

Outside, the lady walked me out of the complex to our driveway. She led me to a police car and placed my things in the back seat. She knelt down to me and questioned, "Do you know where you are going?"

I shook my head, then looked down at the cement in embarrassment.

"You are going to foster care; you will be safe there."

I nodded and said thank you, then climbed into the back seat of the car. I buckled up and looked out the window. Two policemen spoke back and forth in the front seat as I sat quietly in shock. They started the car and drove away. I looked back at what I knew to be home, and the smaller it got, the more emotion I struggled to control. As we rounded the corner, I lost sight and sighed. I felt sick to my stomach, and as scared as a child could be. In an attempt to soothe myself, I kept repeating to myself what Deborah had said: it would all be okay.

Chapter Three

My first foster home placement in Coeur d' Alene was with a couple named Daniel and Laura. The police had taken me ten miles east on the freeway, then exited off what seemed to be a deserted highway. We met Laura and her daughter Crystal at a turnabout off the road. The first time I saw Laura, I remember a small smile crossing my heart. She had long, blond hair that descended down her back. Her kind posture and genuine heart instantly showed and made the pain a little more bearable. As I moved my things into her car, we introduced ourselves, and she told me she was glad I would be staying with her family.

The ride up through the mountains to their log home was quiet. I looked out the window and tried to sort my thoughts. I watched the trees pass by and gazed at the farmland. Numerous turns later, we climbed up a steep dirt road. Once at the end, the car climbed to a plateau, and a beautiful brown home lay in front of me. Daniel was a logger and had built the home from the ground up. Inside the main entrance was a mudroom to my left where I took off my shoes. Snacks and pantry items lined the shelves and I remember being shocked by how much quality food they had. The floors were light brown and glistened from the chandelier lights above. Oak wood lined the walls with swirls of years passed. Bear skin, elk heads, and deer antlers filled the walls. It smelt of cinnamon and tree bark, and I recall every day feeling like the Christmas I had always longed for. They had three horses, a black lab named Sammie, and several chickens.

      The first night I arrived Laura asked me to set the table. Confused, I stood baffled and looked back at her. I asked what she meant, and she explained that each night her family sat at the table and ate dinner together. Since I was now part of the family, I would be joining them. My job was then to help set up the table, which meant laying down the needed utensils and condiments. I look back on this day now recalling the excitement I felt, thinking back to the days when I would watch families through their windows as they laughed with each other passing food around the table. I got to eat dinner with a family. It's such a simple thing to many, but for me, it was a day I will never forget.

Living with Daniel and Laura was the first time I recognized that I had been taken from my mom and placed in foster care. While I was scared of the future, I was comforted by Laura. At night she would pray with me and we had several conversations on the long drives into town.

      Each day before school I collected eggs from the chickens for Laura to wash for breakfast. After eating, Laura would call me to the bathroom to do my hair. I can still feel her soft hands as she brushed my hair then twisted it back row by row. She would section my hair into five parts then twist back the curls, securing them with orange butterfly clips. I had never felt so loved. Part of me felt guilty, like I was cheating on my mom. I felt sad to feel so close to a woman I barely knew and to trust her like I did. These were moments I had not felt with my own mom and it seemed unfair for me to be so happy. Even so, I pushed those negative thoughts to the back of my mind, and enjoyed each moment.

Living with Daniel and Laura brought many new experiences into my life. They were active in their church, and on the weekends we would go to church together as a family. Church was awkward for me sometimes because I didn't know what was going on. The people there were gentle and loving. Some of the women hugged me as we were introduced. No one asked where I came from or how I was part of the family; it didn't matter to them.

Days at Laura's were fun as I always had something to do. Some days after school I would jump on their trampoline while Daniel cut wood outside. When it got dark, Daniel would come jump with me then help me off the side into the grass. We would talk as we walked into the house for dinner. He laughed with me as I told him stories about my day. I recall how it felt to trust a man for the first time, and to not feel uncomfortable when he reached for a hug or placed his hand on my shoulder as he walked by. I wasn't intimidated or scared, I was safe.

Christmas with this family was enchanting. Snow reflected light and filled the house with sparkles. All I could see outside was snow-covered trees and fence posts. On Christmas Eve we sat around the fireplace and ate kettle corn popcorn. Laura made the best popcorn and I am convinced she must have had a special ingredient, because to this day I still cannot find anything like it. Maybe it was simply because she made it. We watched a black and white movie and laughed in unison at the childish jokes. That night, I sat up in bed replaying my day, feeling happy and not wanting to sleep because I didn't want it to end. Eventually my eyes got droopy, and I slipped off into a peaceful sleep.

Christmas Day I woke up to Crystal whispering my name. She had come downstairs to wake me and be the first to wish me a Merry Christmas. I crawled down the bunk bed ladder and followed Crystal as she ran up the stairs to the living room. Everyone sat around the tree in their pajamas. There were flames crackling in the fireplace and an incredible amount of love filled the room. As we opened presents I felt like I was drifting through the clouds. I could not believe I was part of a real family. I got a family for Christmas, and life could not have been better.

As I started my teen years, Laura helped me develop my morals and views on life. I started to realize what a normal family and life was like, and it made me dread the possibility of going back home. I was extremely torn when my caseworker asked if I felt ready to return home. I did not want to go home and was fearful of what would happen to me. I felt loved and safe at Laura's but did not want to hurt my mom. It's a strange feeling to describe. Although my mother didn't protect me from abuse and had been absent for a lot of my childhood, she was still my mother. She had carried me for nine months and given birth to me. She fed me and clothed me. We had an unspeakable bond. While her mothering wasn't perfect, she would always be my mother.

I did not stay with Daniel and Laura long. My mom developed a case plan with the state and agreed to seek help. I was then returned back into her care. I felt an incredible sadness during my last morning with Daniel and Laura. I was starting to identify with my emotions more and had become mature enough to express them. I had a different insight as to how I wanted my life to be and grew courage to stand up more for myself. I knew I would miss Laura's family and the peacefulness I felt in the absence of chaos.

The last morning of my stay Laura came downstairs with a blue Rubbermaid box and helped me pack my things. She hugged me and I cried into her sea of hair. She held me close and promised I could always come see her. She promised she would never forget me. I held her tight when she dropped me off at school. I still can see myself slowly stepping up the sidewalk curb and onto the school pavement. I can still feel my heart drop as I watched her car leaving me behind.

The whole day at school I was distraught and didn't pay attention in class. I watched the clock as I knew once 2:30 came, it was back to reality. I braced myself for anything and started on my trek home.

As I walked the six blocks home I talked aloud to God. I knew now who He was and had developed some faith in my time with Daniel and Laura. I thanked Him for the first time. I thanked Him for letting me experience love and a family. I thanked Him for the memories I had that made me smile. I also asked Him something. I asked Him for a way back out.

Chapter Four

When I arrived home that afternoon, my belongings were already there waiting for me. Things looked the same and as usual; Jeff and my mom were watching T.V. My mom was cracking sunflower seeds, her favorite. She did not have many teeth left, so in an attempt to break the seeds open she would stick her index finger in the roof of her mouth as she bit down. She would sit for hours as she made her way through a full bag. Jeff barely looked up from his program to notice me. I stood for a minute and looked around the room, taking it all back in. This did not feel like home, it felt empty. I sighed deeply and gathered my thoughts. I picked up my bag, threw it over my shoulder, and began my hike up the stairs.

    My room was the same—a mess, but untouched. I didn't try to clean; I was too exhausted to care. I crawled into bed and missed Laura. I imagined myself laughing and eating popcorn. I pictured Daniel coming up the driveway and me waiting anxiously to greet him. I pretended to smell cinnamon and Christmas as I rocked myself back and forth to try to fall asleep. My bed felt foreign and hard. I wrapped my arms around myself and pictured Laura running her hands through my hair as she prayed with me. I rocked and hummed until I managed to finally fall asleep.

    The next day at school I mostly kept to myself. I didn't want to talk and especially did not want anyone to know that I was back with my mom. Midday I was called to the front office. As I walked down the hall, a glimmer of hope passed through me. Maybe the state had changed their minds, and I was going to go back to Laura's house. I could leave today, it wouldn't take me long to pack. I started mapping out my move as I neared the front end of the school. Once I reached the office I was sent to a conference room. I opened the door to an empty room with only a wooden table with chairs around it. A nice-looking lady sat in one of the middle chairs, and seemed excited to meet me. She had long curly hair brown hair that sat past her shoulders. She was wearing a sparkly pink sequin shirt and matching skirt that touched her toes. She stood to greet me, then closed the door.

    The woman introduced herself as Casey and told me she was my new CASA, or Court Appointed Special Advocate. I had no idea what she meant so she explained further. She said when my mom attended court and the judge asked about my welfare, Casey would give the judge her opinion. She would meet with my teachers, doctors and social worker to check in on me. She would come to my school and have lunch with me some days as well as attend my meetings with the state regarding my mom's case plan. She told me she was there especially for me and that her main goal was to keep me safe and healthy. At the age of thirteen she did not feel it was in my best interest for me to be in court for the hearings regarding my placement, although I sometimes had that choice. She had a gentle demeanor and was very kind. I did not know it at the time, but she would become one of the most influential people in my life.

My life at home with my mom, Jeff, and Amanda stayed the same as before. I tried to numb myself to it, but now that I knew different, I started to fight back. Jeff and I never grew to like each other, and the abuse continued.

My sister had been sent to rehab while I was gone. She had gotten pretty deep into drugs and was suspended from school. She became unruly and was sent away to get help. Every once in a while I would get a letter from her. In the letters she would tell me what she was learning in treatment and her plans for when she got out. She told me she wanted to be a better person and was going to go back to school. The night she came home we all went out to eat at a Chinese restaurant. Amanda began to talk about how glad she was to be home and how she disliked the rehab she was in. When I went back to the buffet for seconds she made a joke about my weight. We started arguing and I was discouraged that she seemed to be the same as when she left. I was angry and told her that she wasn't my real sister. We only shared the same mother but at that moment I felt we shared nothing. We argued at the table until Jeff was irritated and grabbed me by the arm. He led me out of the restaurant into the parking lot toward our Jeep. He shoved me around the side of the car facing away from the restaurant and lowered his face down to mine. He shamed me for fighting with Amanda on her first night home and told me when we were home I was going to get it. He proceeded to tell me to keep my mouth shut until we got home and to go directly to the garage. I followed behind him back into the restaurant and kept quiet for the rest of the meal. I pushed my food around my plate and wondered exactly what he would do to me. I felt sick to my stomach the rest of the night, contemplating what my punishment was going to be. When we got home I went straight for the garage and sat there for three hours while he worked on his Jeep. I waited, frightened, as he took his time working under the hood. He worked leisurely as I sat anxiously awaiting, my fear growing by the minute. Finally, he rubbed his cracked hands on a dirty cloth and approached me. First, he grabbed my wrist and pulled me up from the couch I was sitting on. He then told me to take my pants to my knees and bend over so he could spank me. I felt ashamed to have my pants off and was juggling which would be worse: that or once he hit me. I tried to be strong; I knew I could endure the pain as I had many times before. I sobbed to myself as he threw each blow. The force of his swing almost caused me to stumble, but I caught myself. I refrained from begging, knowing it would only excite him more. As the pain intensified, I began to lose control and my sobs became louder. A combination of shame and stinging just about brought me to my knees. I don't remember how he decided to stop. I don't even remember when he did. I only remember pulling up my pants and scooting away as fast as my body would allow. Once outside the garage, I limped to the apartment and made my way upstairs to my room. In bed I laid on my stomach as my backside hurt too much. Feeling only comfort from familiarity, I cried myself to sleep.

    I am still unsure today why I was placed back at my mother's. While I know my mom agreed to a case plan, I also know she did not fully comply with it. Jeff refused to come to meetings and made no effort initially to get me back. I was confused as to why I was uprooted from a loving home, and put back into the same unhealthy, unsafe situation. Around this time my mom had started seeing a counselor and psychiatrist and was diagnosed with Paranoid Schizophrenia and extreme depression. The counselor said that because of trauma she had suffered as a child, her brain never matured past that of a teenager's. They also said she heard voices that told her to do things. I started to learn about these conditions in school and it helped me to be more empathetic toward her and less angry. Despite her counseling and diagnosis, nothing changed. A few months later, our neighbors heard Jeff hitting me in the garage again and they called the police. Only then I was placed back in foster care.

Chapter Five

The second time I was removed from home I had a better understanding of what was going on, but this time Casey was there for me during the process. My second foster care placement was in a group home. I called Casey often, and told her about the new home I was in. I shared with her my feelings about being taken away and how I was settling in. She listened closely and asked a lot of questions. It was nice to have someone to talk to and it seemed as though Casey enjoyed listening to me. She always answered my phone calls and never rushed me through what I had to say. She started coming to the group home to have lunch with me or spend time together after dinner. We would often go down to the basement where it was quiet as she asked me questions about visits I had with my mom. She also questioned me on how I felt living in the group home.

The group home was structured similarly to my idea of a boarding school. It was run by all women, known as house moms. Privileges were split into levels that I had to earn by obeying the rules, doing chores, and listening to staff. The first level was called "obbs," short for observation. On this level you could not go anywhere alone, except the bathroom. This system was established to keep the children safe and the house in order. The house moms would hold house meetings and decide whether or not to move a child up or down a level. The highest level was level four. On this level you could go to friends' houses, and had freedom to roam around the house alone.

I had multiple conflicts with two house moms. It was hard for me to take direction from women who seemed to control me without empathy. It was different at home because I expected that, but not here. I wanted to go back to Daniel and Laura's, but they were no longer taking in foster children. I stood up for myself when I felt I was being mistreated and as a result I would get in more trouble for being disrespectful. Several times I lost my level status. I started to get discouraged as I saw other children get adopted or returned to their families. I started putting on more weight and was devastated to find I had contracted head lice. For months we treated my hair, combed out all we could and kept my hair in a shower cap. In an effort to not contaminate the other kids I had to sometimes sit at a different table and was not allowed in certain areas. Looking back now I understand why, although at the time it increased my feelings of inadequacy. I started to slip deep into depression and shut people out. I convinced myself no one wanted me and I didn't deserve a family. When my desperation reached its peak I decided the best thing would be to end my life.

I gathered all of my pictures and said my goodbyes. I grieved over everything painful, and apologized in advance for what I was about to do. I didn't want to die but I did not want to live either. I accepted this as the best option for me and that everyone would be better off. I shuffled through my dresser until I found my light pink razor. I broke the top into pieces and freed the blades from the plastic. Then I grabbed my blanket and curled up in the corner. Discouraged and hopeless, I prepared myself. I cried out in unfairness and regret, and began what was my only way out. I convinced myself it would be better to feel nothing than to feel this. I summoned up enough courage to grip the blade in my right hand, and met it with my left wrist. I slowly started to pierce the skin and think of nothingness.

As the blade began its journey across my skin, I heard footsteps down the hall. Startled and scared, I ran and jumped in bed and pulled the covers over my face. The house moms were doing their nightly checks and they could not catch me. I faked being asleep as the house mom for that day opened the door. I inhaled slowly and made sure my chest rose so she would not inspect further. She checked the other children then turned off all the hallway lights and kept my door open. Not wanting to be caught, I decided I would have to try again another day.

After being at the group home for six months I started to bond with the staff. Some would read to me, and play with my hair until I fell asleep. Others would sneak in my room in the middle of the night and tell me stories or ask me about my day. The evening staff seemed to understand I was struggling and took me under their wing to help me during my transition into my teens. There were a lot of other children at this home, and I got to feel what it was like to be a big sister. I would do crafts with them and play in the back yard. I realized I was going to be there for a while and I should make the best of it. My conflicts with the staff continued, but I looked forward to seeing the staff that took extra care of me. As the other foster kids moved on, whether they were adopted or went back home, I learned to become happy for them.

This home was meant to be a temporary placement, but I stayed there for over fourteen months. It was hard to place me in a home because most foster parents prefer to take in little children over teenagers. My mom seemed disappointed that I was not coming home, though her husband did not want me there either. She was placed in a situation where she had to choose between her husband or her child. I told Casey I did not want to go home as long as he was there and that I did not feel safe. Casey would tell the court or my caseworker who reported to the court, and they would then inform my mom. When my mom came to visit me in the group home, although I loved seeing her, it was exceptionally emotional. She would ask me why I didn't want to come home and it was hard for me tell her why. It was painful to see the sadness in her eyes. I started experiencing a great deal of guilt. After her visits I would stand outside and half-smile and wave as she left. I could see the tears and hopelessness in her eyes as she left me behind. Then I would go inside and break down. I thought that maybe I was just being selfish, and maybe I was strong enough now to handle Jeff and Amanda. I wasn't.

The guilt got worse and created more tension between my mom and I. We started to fight over our phone visits. She said I was an ungrateful little brat. I told her it wasn't her, and that if she left Jeff I would say I wanted to come home. I told her I was scared of him and just wanted him to leave. The stress of fighting with my mom caused my grades to slip and school became more of a burden than an escape. My teachers encouraged me to stay focused, but life outside of school took all the energy I had.

During my time at the group home, I became good friends with a girl at school named Whitney. One day after class I went home with her and met her parents,

Scott and Pamela. Scott was a doctor and Pamela stayed home with the children. The family attended the church across from the group home, so I started attending with them on Sundays.

Scott and Pamela became very supportive role models to me. They started including me in their family activities and spent a lot of time getting to know me. Scott purchased a guitar for me so I could learn to play. Pamela picked me up from school some days and I would tag along as she ran errands and then go home with her. I started to love this family, and felt comfortable like I had at Laura's. I began to spend more and more time with them, and even spent some holidays with them and their relatives. Scott and Pamela decided to take foster care classes so they could take me in permanently. I was ecstatic; I had found a family!

At this time my teeth were bothering me. My mouth was overcrowded with extra teeth, and I was in desperate need of braces. I was on the Medicaid waiting list, but most likely I would turn eighteen and age out of the system before they got to me. Scott and Pamela took this upon themselves, and set an appointment for me to get braces. They purchased the braces for me, and Scott went to the dentist with me and held my hand. We bonded as we spent more time together and he became a father figure to me. I looked up to him as a doctor, and his accomplishments encouraged me to do well in school so I too could be successful one day.

I remained at the group home for a little while longer and had hopes of going to live with Scott and Pamela. But as time went on, Scott and Pamela started coming around less and their daughter Whitney starting to withdraw from the youth group. She seemed sad and distant. When I asked her what was wrong, she cried as she told me her parents were talking about getting a divorce. I was shocked and had no idea they were having troubles. They seemed like the perfect family to me. Later, Scott and Pamela told me they were in fact getting a divorce, and were sad that they wouldn't be able to take me after all. I was dismayed and hurt, but disbelief kept me from processing the reality of what their divorce really would mean to our relationship. It meant I no longer got to go live with them and I didn't get to be a part of their family. I stayed at the group home a little while longer. Then, after fourteen long months, the judge decided to send me back home to my mom.

Chapter Six

Going back to my mom's house this time was strange. We really didn't know what to say to each other or how to deal with me being away in foster care for so long. Because we hadn't had many visits together, we didn't have time to build a relationship so that when I did return home we could have worked on being healthy. She strained to get off drugs, but relapsed several times. She found it difficult to give up what she had become accustomed to. I feel as though drugs comforted her and provided an escape. Jeff saw no value in becoming clean, especially since that heightened the chances of me being reunited with my mom.

While I was away at the group home my mother had moved. The new place was a single family home located downtown. There was a big tree in the front yard with bulky, sprawling branches. Moving back in with my mom meant I had to switch middle schools, and I found it difficult to leave behind my friends and teachers. However, there were some positive things about my new school. It was close to home so I walked each morning to and from school. I made friends quickly and became friends with the school janitor, who was also our neighbor.

Though I made new friends, school still had its obstacles. I had been diagnosed with a heart murmur at birth and asthma as a young child, and one day during gym class I got sick from overexertion. After that day I wasn't allowed to participate in gym class. Over time this made losing weight more difficult, and I grew larger as the days passed. At home, we did not eat together as a family, and many nights I was left to fend for myself. Lack of choices for healthy food caused me to gain more weight. My mom was diabetic and struggled to stay away from sugars, even though she knew how it could harm her. Our house was filled with treats and candy, and I recall many dinners of Top Ramen and Reese's candy. Even though I had friends, I was still being bullied for my weight. Not being able to participate in physical activities in school seemed to make my health poorer and set me apart from the other students.

As I struggled to adapt to the new changes in my life, my relationship with my sister stayed the same. We rarely spoke, and the tension grew. She was gone most days, fishing with her boyfriend or hanging out with her friends. Then, at the age of sixteen, she found out she was pregnant. She was shocked but excited, and she decided to keep the child and move out on her own. At seventeen she was emancipated and moved out with her boyfriend shortly before her son was born. He was a healthy, happy baby and for the first time in a long time, I felt a bond with her as I cradled him in my arms. I smile at the thought of holding him, so fragile and reliant on my support. I was proud of Amanda; she had created a little miracle.

I wondered what life would look like for this new baby. Would his innocence cause my sister to be more patient and less violent, or would she continue life as she had before he was born?

Living at home again brought the same challenges as before, but I tried to find ways to deal with them. Jeff and I continued to quarrel, and he proceeded to be abusive. As I got older, his tactics changed. One disagreement ended with me cornered in the kitchen. I recall him shouting at me, and my resentment growing. Trapped, I held steady, though I knew something was about to hurt. After yelling obscenities in my face, his spit smothering me, he reached for my wrist. I attempted to pull away from him, but his strength overpowered me. He turned on the sink water till it was scalding and stuck my hand in the water that had accumulated in the sink below. His words were irrelevant, and all I could think to do was scream. I splashed my hand away as he held it down, steam flowing up from the contact. He snickered as I tried to get away. Once his need to fulfill his foolish pride subsided, he let me go. I ran out the back door and started my trek to school. It was 6:55 in the morning. Just one hour and five minutes until school was open.

Often times I would walk to school early in the morning to talk to my teachers about life at home. Having someone to turn to was a luxury I was not accustomed to. The school counselor saw me in her office, and it was a safe place for me to talk about my feelings. Up until that point I had not really thought about how my home life was affecting me emotionally. When you are raised in chaos, you assume that is what normality looks like. Counseling helped me identify my feelings and to see what healthy boundaries and relationships looked like. It helped me to differentiate between what was my normal, and what was actually normal. Sometimes it helped me to not feel so guilty for wanting a better quality of life. However, when Casey and my social worker asked me about where I wanted to live, I struggled with my emotions. I debated on what to say to them. I loved my mom, but things had not changed at home. I had become less sensitive to the physical abuse and more hurt by the emotional. Jeff had grown more spiteful of me as time went on and he never failed to remind me. His words cut and slashed me as he said the most hurtful things he could think of. Why was he out to get me? Eventually I felt as though I was bleeding from the inside out. I started to lose the little hope I had left.

With the continued drug use at home and the physical abuse from Jeff, I reached the point where hopelessness started to drown me, and I searched for an escape. Thinking I could do better on my own, I started to plan my getaway. I had plans of getting my own place and decorating it with vanilla sugar candles and decorative centerpieces. I envisioned coming home and reading a book on the couch with a fluffy blanket, warm, safe, and welcome.

One night I tried to run away. Bent on sour emotions, I had not planned thoroughly but acted rather on a whim. Equipped with the bare necessities, I headed for the door. Jeff awoke to the screen door as it slammed shut. Knowing he heard me, I ran. I hid in the bushes of a neighbor's house, fearing he would look for me running. As I peered through the bushes, I waited for my opportunity to run. He stood on the porch, a phone glued to his ear. Who was he calling? I sat and waited for him to go inside, but he stood still. I looked around to see if I could escape without him hearing or seeing me, but decided to stay put. Thoughts ran through my head, and suddenly I saw red and blue lights flash as a cruiser pulled into our driveway. It didn't take long for the police to discover me beneath the bushes and walk me home.

My yearning for positive change continued to grow. I could hardly wait to turn eighteen and be on my own. I relied on my teachers at school for emotional support as I navigated through my teens alone. My English teacher suggested I try writing my thoughts down through poetry. I enjoyed finding new words to rhyme with what I was trying to say. I felt a sense of relief once I expressed my thoughts on paper. Poetry became art, and I found a hidden passion for words. I wrote almost every day and found comfort in putting my feelings into words. There was something therapeutic about writing it down. Unlike life, I could put the pencil down when I was done. I could write on my own terms, it was just me and the paper. I wished writing down the words meant I could throw away my situation like I did a piece I didn't like. Regrettably, neither school nor poetry took away what was still happening at home. While I continued to write, it didn't take the pain away. Lost, confused, and feeling like I was out of options, I resorted back to suicide.

My sister was the one who walked in on me. Humiliated, I lied and said I was not serious about the attempt. Amanda knew better, and cumulatively she and my mom decided to bring me to the emergency room. After being physically cleared, I was evaluated by a child psychiatrist. I was then sent to a children's psychiatric hospital.

My first night in the hospital I was placed in a white room. All the surfaces were covered with padding and I was checked on each hour. Later, I was relocated to a regular room where I had a roommate. I recollect reading most of the day, as it was the only choice I had other than thinking. I certainly did not want to have that much time to just think. When I was at the hospital Casey came to visit and pray with me. She promised me that she would do her best to get me back out of my mom's house. She said she would consistently report to the judge that it was not a safe place for me and that my suicide attempt clearly proved the danger I was in. I wasn't safe with my mother, not just physically, but mentally as well.

A week into my stay, my mom came to visit. I watched as she exited her car and approached the building. I began to feel nervous as I did not know what to say. The first few words were awkward as I struggled to explain myself. I sat dressed in scrubs and lowered my head in shame as I muttered "I'm sorry" through my tears. My mom started crying, and guilt struck my heart. I swallowed salt and the devastation in her eyes haunted me. She reached out and handed me a teddy bear. I clung to it for dear life, appreciating something soft.

When the visit was over a staff member escorted my mom to the door. As I had many times before, I watched her leave. The sound of keys and metal sent a chill down my spine as the staff member locked my mother out. Gravity took hold of my tears, and they fell to the floor. I clenched my bear, and the moment she was out of sight I ran down the hallway to my room as fast as my feet would allow. I wanted to cry alone. My face was buried in the bear, partially for comfort and partly because of shame. I approached my room and crawled onto the bed. Curled up in a fetal position I cried out in despair. I was emotionally exhausted. Something had to change.

I decided that day, after Casey's recommendation, that I wanted to write a letter to the judge. I needed to tell him how I felt about living at home with my mom. I couldn't handle not only the abuse, but the emotional state of guilt that I had. I felt remorseful for wanting better. It was difficult to articulate my thoughts, as I had many conflicting feelings. I attempted to express that this was in my best interest, and that the constant instability contributed to my suicidal feelings. I felt it was my only way out. I explained that I wanted to live, just not like this. Casey read the letter, made some edits, then delivered it to the judge. He decided to remove me and place me back into foster care.

    While I was still in the hospital I received a visit from a lady named Angela. She told me that she was going to be my new foster mom. She and her husband Keith lived in Sandpoint, Idaho, which is about thirty miles from Coeur d'Alene. Angela communicated to me that they had never been foster parents before, and I could see the excitement in her eyes. I was going to be their first and only child. Her husband Keith was a youth pastor. Angela had numerous ideas to welcome me into their home. As she described their house, she asked what theme I wanted to do for my room. My eyes lit up as I told her of my love for palm trees, and my dream to go to Hawaii one day. We compiled a bundle of ideas, including making my bedpost into palm trees, and painting the walls. A small glimmer of hope lit up, but I did not allow myself to get too excited.

Chapter Seven

Angela and Keith welcomed me with open arms. We all worked through the awkwardness of the new situation at the same pace. Angela was more of a free spirit, and she gave me room to be myself. After school I would come home and watch movies that Angela had set out for me. I started high school at Sandpoint High and joined the drama club. I auditioned for a play and landed the role of a bum in the play "Little Shop of Horrors."

I was open with them about the trials I faced in other homes and why they did not work out. I stressed to Angela my fear of men, and asked that she never leave me alone with Keith. At this time, I was extremely distrustful of men, except for Daniel and Scott. I was still hurt that the two men I did trust were no longer a part of my life, and their absence heightened my sensitivity. I was not ready to be hurt again. I asked if Angela would be the one to take me to school and my drama practices, and she seemed to understand.

Angela and Keith loved on me as I attempted to figure out who I was. Besides the occasional disagreement, things were going quite well. Angela was busy with work, and Keith spent a great deal of time at the church. The space allowed me to not feel suffocated, and I enjoyed my freedom, and their trust.

Things changed when Angela had to leave for a business trip for a week. Daniel was left to care for me and take me to and from school. He made every effort to earn my trust, and he gave me no reason not to trust him. Sadly, I still had many issues from my past and I pushed him away. One evening at a drive-through, I became fearful sitting alone in the car with him. An argument started, and once I had jumped out of the car, I did what I thought was best. I ran. I ended up on a bridge near the outskirts of the city, unaware of what to do next. I remember that day on the bridge, I was looking out over the water thinking about what was coming next. The water soothed me and my thoughts became clearer. My cluster of thoughts narrowed down to one: Where would I go now?

After leaving the home of Angela and Keith, I was once again in need of help. As my CASA, Casey had become deeply involved in my life. She was present at all of my meetings, hearings and appointments. She made more frequent house visits and over time we grew closer. She became more than my advocate and at the time was one of the few people I trusted and could count on. As I navigated through different placements, it became difficult for Casey to watch me go through the emotional turmoil of starting over so frequently. In an effort to protect me and provide stability, Casey decided to quit her job as a CASA so that she and her husband James could become my legal guardians. This was a dream come true as Casey was one of the few consistent people in my life.

I lived with Casey and James for a year and a half, which was my longest placement. By this time I was almost sixteen, and I had been in and out of foster care since I was seven. During that period I had attended six different schools. I still struggled with my weight, and was consequently bullied. I did make friends, but it was easier to keep to myself.

The time I spent with this family was the most influential on my character. Casey had a strong Jewish faith and she showed me her beliefs through her lifestyle. Part of what she taught me was how to be a homemaker. She taught me how to sew, cook and clean, and explained the importance of knowing how to take care of a family. She invited me to celebrate the Sabbath with her and James, and from Friday at sunset to Saturday evening we rested and read the Bible. We would make all of our food days before as part of preparing for the Sabbath. The Sabbath days were special, so we would dress up and have Shabbat dinner around the table. James would wear his special black Stetson hat and Casey wore a beaded lace head covering. After being with them for a while, I got my very own lavender yamaka. I felt like I was part of the family once I received my yamaka and it was a milestone in my relationship with Casey and James.

One of my favorite memories at Casey's home was during bedtime with her puppy, Diamond. I reminisce waking up next to Diamond with Casey rubbing my back and brushing the hair off my face. Initially Diamond was scared of me, and it took time for her to warm up. After a few short days of me hounding her to let me pet her, she caved. I followed her everywhere and pet her whenever she wasn't looking. We became inseparable, and she slept next to me every night. I would lie on my side and place her in my arms. The rhythm of her heartbeat was music to my ears. I loved to watch as her eyes filled with contentment and she fell asleep.

At night, Casey would call Diamond into my room, and the three of us would huddle as Casey prayed over me. She ran her hands along my back, and soothed me until I was able to fall asleep. Truly then, was I able to see her love for me. I was not a case, I was a child.

I also began to establish a relationship with Casey's husband James. I had become more comfortable around men and that helped in my relationship with James. In the summer he did motocross racing. I would go to the tracks with him sometimes and watch him ride. He had a lot of little projects around the house and I liked to help him with them. He assigned me my own chores and I was able to learn how to clean and do yard work. Casey helped me with my homework, and packed my lunch each day for school. In the morning James would walk me to the bus stop before he left for work. Life started to seem normal.

Shortly after my sixteenth birthday, I received a call around five in the morning from my sister, whom I seldom spoke to. Casey answered the call from another room and tried to make out the words coming from the other end. She walked into my room, her face pale as she handed the phone to me. I remember the conversation almost exactly.

Amanda was sobbing when I picked up the phone and she had a hard time speaking. She stumbled through the words, "Kaila....it's mom."

"What? What happened?" I asked.

She was hysterical, her loud weeping making her words difficult to understand. Panic set in as thoughts raced my mind, and again I questioned her.

Her response remained the same.

"Kaila, it's mom, it's mom."

I said, "What? What's wrong? Did she get into a car accident?" I could hear my sister breathing heavily in the background as she set the phone down briefly to gather herself. I sat up out of bed and realized my face was wet with tears. My heart sank to the bottom of my chest and I knew something was horribly wrong. Fear kept me from questioning more and I was scared of what was to come next. Moments passed, then she said the worst three words I had ever heard. "Kaila--mom's dead."

Shock hit me like a ton of bricks, and my heart shattered in that moment. Denial took over and I insisted it was a joke. How could she die? She was thirty-eight! I buried my head in my hands and shock wrapped my veins and caused my blood to rush. I became hot then cold and confused. I rocked myself back and forth, trying to comprehend what had just happened. I needed something. I needed something to take away the pain, it was too unbearable. How could she be gone? I just spoke to her two days earlier. She was going to come visit me, she promised! In rhythmic motion I rocked, cried, rocked, cried until Casey coaxed me to the car. As I walked into the living room James emerged from the bedroom wearing his pajamas and slippers. On his head he wore his Stetson top hat, the one he wore for special occasions. I recall his hat standing out to me as it cemented how serious the situation was.

The ten minute drive to the hospital is all a blur to me now. I am sure Casey comforted me as best she could. Upon arrival we found that my mom's body had already been moved. We drove the short distance to my grandparents' house where the family had gathered. No one looked up as I entered, and I knew that I had been alienated for 'choosing to be in foster care'. For some reason I thought differences could be set aside for a time such as this. A few hugs were shared, and Amanda and I embraced. She told Casey my mom's body had been placed in the funeral home four blocks away, and Jeff was working on the details.

We drove to the funeral home in silence. The cold, brown building seemed eerie to me, and I was unsure of whether I wanted to go inside. Casey and James spoke to the receptionist as I waited in the lobby, not knowing what to expect. A tall, thin, white-haired man gently apologized for my loss. He led me down the hall to a room on the right. He told me to take my time, and he would be at the front desk should I need anything. Should I need anything? What could I possibly need at that point other than the one thing he couldn't give me? My mother.

Casey and James explained to me that my mom was in the room, and if I wanted to I could say goodbye. Unsure of how this worked I simply nodded. They waited on the bench outside the room for me. As I opened the door, I proceeded with caution. My eyes were heavy, and I struggled to focus. The room was plain, with no decorations to distract me from the agony of what was to come next. There was nothing that could have helped at that moment, as if a bundle of fake flowers and a few scenic pictures would make things more bearable.

My mom's body was lying on a metal table. It looked like a scene from a horror film. She was held together in a plastic bag. I sobbed as reality set in. Looking down I saw her pale face and blue lips; she was empty. She was gone. Dried blood sat in the corners of her ears and the space between her nose and mouth. Her neck had been cut severely from the tracheotomy performed by the EMT who had tried to save her, and the blood had dried with her hair stuck to it. I reached for her hand and found it deep within the bag. Unable to reach it, I placed my hand gently on her forehead. I sobbed as I apologized for everything I had done. I had been ungrateful. I could have been stronger. I could have handled Jeff and Amanda. What kind of daughter was I? This was my fault. I pleaded with her to come back, not to leave me. I insisted I needed her and that I couldn't do life without her. She lay motionless and cold, and I knew she was gone. My mother was gone. I leaned down to kiss her forehead and was surprised to be met with a cold thud. I broke. Every ounce of pain I had ever felt attacked my heart, and the grief was unbearable. Every part of my body shut down and it became difficult to stand. My sobs turned to shrieks as the pain grew. I cried out as I put my hands on my knees to catch my breath. I was in disbelief, shock. Hearing my cries, Casey rushed through the door. She ran over to me and after seeing my mother, she covered my eyes and led me out the room. I was not ready to leave, I was not ready to let go. I hadn't told her I loved her. I hadn't told her goodbye. Did she know I was sorry? Did she know I didn't blame her? What have I done?

Casey reasoned with me to go to the car. Exhausted, I agreed and she helped me outside. The bright light outside stung my eyes as we left the dark building. The car was parked out front and she motioned me in as she opened the back door. I crawled in and fell to my side, where I wept myself to sleep.

Two days later I said goodbye to my mother. Even though we didn't have much contact with my mother's parents, Donald and Joyce, they were both at my mother's service. During the service everyone took a moment to share memories of my mom. Most spoke of her big heart and childlike personality. When it was my turn, I slowly walked to the front of the room. I observed the twenty or so people looking at me as they ate their fried chicken, corn, and potato salad. Jeff was unable to afford a funeral service so he rented out the basement of a rundown church. I look back now, upset he didn't find a way to come up with money to have a better service for her. I turned around a framed picture of my mom that I was clutching in my weak hands. It was all I had left of her. I cried through trying to say something, anything that would give her life value. I spoke of her best feature, her heart. I shared memories of my mom giving the neighborhood kids our Easter eggs because they could not afford any. She oftentimes gave away our food, money, and belongings, even when we needed them. She liked to help people, she was selfless in that way. I said I loved her, and how I missed her so much already. No words seemed to justify what I truly felt.

After the devastation set in, I slipped into a deep depression. Pain, guilt, and grief suffocated me as I tried to make it through one day at a time. Casey took me out of school to grieve for a week, for which I was thankful. I locked myself in my room, and occasionally surfaced to use the restroom or grab enough food rations to get me by. In an attempt to maintain normality, Casey expected me to continue with life as I had before. I wanted to be left alone and did not want to come out to do my chores. I did not want to eat dinner at the table, and would have happily starved so I could be alone. I was drowning in my misery, and it seemed like the appropriate and only response. Casey continued to push me to do my chores, and once I was back in school, to do my homework. I couldn't have cared less about school, and even less about chores. The further I slipped into depression, the more I pushed Casey away. I wanted to be alone. I wanted nothing to do with anyone. I had no idea how to handle such pain, but I was not about to numb it with tedious tasks such as dishes.

Eventually, the disruption turned to a point of no return. In distancing myself, I caused everyone to feel uncomfortable and I no longer felt welcome. I felt that working through my grief was destroying their family. I decided it was best to leave. As painful as it was, I did not want to create chaos for them after they had opened their home to me. I needed time to grieve. I needed time.

A friend's parents offered to take me in until I turned eighteen. It took two weeks for the judge to sign the paperwork to give me away. This time was different, I was not going to start over. I focused on my eighteenth birthday and couldn't wait to run. Somewhere in the back of my mind I thought I could run far enough that the pain couldn't reach me.

My final placement seems like a speck of sand in the shore of my life. I stayed briefly, making as little connections as possible. By this time I learned that love creates vulnerability, and vulnerability opens the door for pain. My door was shut. I had no heart left to give. I was broken.

November thirtieth came, and my birthday was merely a celebration of freedom. As I had many times before, I packed my things into my blue Rubbermaid box and prepared for my next stop. Alone, I was finally ready to start over again.

Chapter Eight

Try and remember the day you left home for the first time. What things did you take with you? Clothes, a computer, books, money….What tools did you have to aid you through the transition? Did you have the ability to balance a checkbook, or skills such as sewing or maintaining a budget? Did you leave knowing you always had a resting spot if things didn't pan out?

Turning eighteen is a different process for youth in foster care. According to the Pew Charitable Trust Report, six out of ten foster children who leave foster care at eighteen will likely be homeless, incarcerated or dead by the age of twenty. Many leave care without healthy connections, or resources to aid them into becoming productive, educated adults. When a child reaches a set age (states vary) then the state is no longer their legal guardian, and they "age out" of the system. When I turned eighteen, I was not in close connection with my state caseworker. I had not been educated on the many resources available for me once leaving the system, mostly financial. I attempted to make it on my own and worked two jobs while trying to complete high school. Scott (who had tried to take me in when I was at the group home) and his new wife Loretta let me live with them until I graduated. If it had not been for them I most likely would have dropped out in order to work more. Scott showed me the value of an education and encouraged me to look at colleges. I had held back from looking into schools because I was fearful I would not be able to afford it, but Scott encouraged me to apply for aid and offered to help me in any way he could. With his encouragement and support I enrolled in my first class in the fall of 2009.

Once in school, I started to understand that the world was at my fingertips. I started to think more positively and was optimistic that I could become anything I wanted to. I started to find my joy again in learning, and started to have hope for my future. My passion for school that had been dimmed slowly started to shine again.

Once I was able to afford my own apartment, I moved out of Scott and Loretta's house. My first apartment was an older home that had been converted into apartments. It was dark red, and placed not too far from a park. I can still recall how wonderful it felt to sign my first lease! Upon getting my keys, I went to the Department of Health and Welfare to see if they had any assistance they could offer me. I was in need of all household amenities. A caseworker informed me that she would look into resources to see what was available for my age bracket, but said I was eligible for a Lifestart kit. She handed me a large Rubbermaid box, and I toted it out to my car. Once at my apartment I sat on the living room floor, excited to finally have my own home. No one could move me, kick me out or make me feel unwelcome. I smiled, thinking how different my life was going to be from that moment on. I pulled the box near me, and remembered my last morning with Laura when she helped me pack my things into the same Rubbermaid box. I sighed deeply then pulled the box near me and broke the tie holding it closed. Inside I found pots and pans, matching dishes, towels, a blanket, a flashlight, a tool kit, and a letter in the bottom saying that the Lifestart kit was from an organization called The Christmas Box House International. There was also a book, *The Five Lessons a Millionaire Taught Me About Life and Wealth* by a man named Richard Paul Evans. I recall thinking, "Somebody thought of me in my situation? Somebody cared enough to donate things to get me started with my life?"

Incredibly moved by this random act of kindness, I decided to reach out to Richard and his organization to thank them. The box was not simply filled with physical items, it was filled with hope. Up until that point, Rubbermaid boxes were symbolic of a failed placement. They reminded me of leaving Laura's. Having the same box filled with encouragement hit home for me. It was emblematic for the change in my life that was occurring.

Upon calling the organization, I was put in contact with Jenna, Richard's daughter and writing assistant. After exchanging a few short sentences, I felt like I had known her for years. She asked me questions about how I had gotten the box, and a little about my story. We talked about foster care, the death of my mom, and my hopes for my college career. At the end of our conversation, Jenna informed me that Richard may call me with questions for feedback, as I was the first recipient they had heard from.

Within the next few days, Richard called me. His kind voice and gentle demeanor explained how he could have sent the box. Wanting to meet me and hear more of my story, Richard flew me to his home in Salt Lake City. I got to meet his family and partake in a video that helped raise awareness of the adversities youth face when "aging" out of care.

The day I spent with Richard and his family was the encouragement I needed and a push in the right direction. Seeing how he believed in me, and how he cared about children he didn't even know, made me want to be a better person. I wanted to be like him and give hope to others.

Over the years Richard and I stayed in contact. He called to check in on me and encourage me in my endeavors. In 2011, Richard was visiting Coeur d Alene while writing the second book in his series *The Walk*. In this series a man is devastated when his wife suddenly dies and he loses his home, business and property all around the same time. To process his loss he walks from Seattle, Washington to Key West, Florida. Richard and his daughter Jenna were traveling along the route the character was walking so they could write about real places and experiences. Around this time, I hadn't spoke to him for a while and thought I should email him and let him know how I was doing. I had no idea he was in Coeur d' Alene and had been thinking of me too. After reading my email, he called me and we met up for lunch. At lunch we caught up and he told about his most recent book series. He explained the character, his story, and how he traveled from one side of the country to the other. He asked me if I would like to be a character in the second book of the series, *Miles to Go*. I was honored that he thought of me and happily agreed. He said he would use my real name and parts of my real story. He also asked that I write my account of what it was like being a foster child and going through the system. It was then that *Out of the Darkness* was born.

Chapter Nine

Of course, life didn't end then. Really, it began. I had time to figure out where I wanted to go with life, but had no idea where to start. In the last ten years, Jeff and both of his parents have passed, as well as both of my mom's parents and one of my best friends. I dealt with a large number of deaths in a short amount of time, and it left me with little time to truly grieve over my mom. Part of me was still in denial. I had not fully understood how *gone* she was until I was much older. I will be honest and say that the first three years after her death were tough. I floated from place to place, and hadn't established any roots. I drifted through life, hoping for a change, but making no effort to do something to start the process. I had goals and dreams, but the scars from my childhood left me bare. I had doubts that dreams could come true for people like me, but I had numerous people in my life encouraging me otherwise. I stayed in touch with Casey, and Loretta and Scott. After I had moved out of Scott and Loretta's house, I reconnected with Scott's former wife Pamela. Pamela apologized that things didn't work out before. She expressed that she still loved me and wanted to be in my life for good, so we re-established a relationship. My teachers Lynn, Leslie, and Martha all have lunch with me each year and check in on my progress. After writing my story, I found healing in doing so. Writing it down set me free. I sat the pain, heartache, shame and guilt on the weight of the paper. I no longer needed to carry it. I had to let go. I had to change my life, and somehow break the cycle of abuse and disorder in my family. That is why I have made it my career choice to help others that have gone through similar trials.

In 2012, I graduated from college with my Associate degree. I am currently in my senior year of college majoring in Business Administration with a double minor in Justice Studies and Communication. I plan on attending law school or obtaining an MBA with an emphasis in Human Resources.

I never dreamt that my past would be so much of who I am today. Telling my story to promote awareness and advocacy for children in the foster system has helped shape me into the woman I am. It has also opened up many doors for me. In 2013, I was appointed by the Governor of Idaho to serve a three-year term on The Juvenile Justice Commission. As a full voting member of the commission I have the unique opportunity to help regulate Juvenile Justice activities and policies through the state of Idaho. I feel honored to be a part of the change that is happening in my state. Through serving on this Commission I have grown as a young woman professionally and emotionally. I have learned how to articulate my thoughts in a professional manner, and can articulate and express my thoughts regarding the system in a healthy way. I have more recently been appointed to serve a four year term on The Governor's Task Force for Children at Risk. In addition to the commission, I am also a member of the Idaho Foster Youth Advisory Board. This board is compiled of youth throughout the state who have been or are currently in foster care. We travel around the state and participate in Pride Panels. In these panels we share our experiences, both good and bad, in an effort to educate, advocate, and reform foster youth policy. We speak at police stations, government meetings, foster parent trainings, and child advocacy conferences. All of our time is volunteered, and it is equipping us to be leaders in our community and nation. We are currently working on a Foster Child's Bill of Rights, as well as a Sibling's Bill of Rights.

My experiences as a child are the only reason I am able to be a part of this board. I understand that we cannot change the fact that youth will be placed in foster care, but find hope in knowing we can change the process for them once they arrive. Through my work in the community I have seen the foster system in Idaho slowly improving, and more resources, connections, and options are available to youth in care. It makes me happy to know that future generations will be better equipped to beat the odds.

In September of 2014 I moved to Washington, D.C. for four months to serve as a Congressional Intern for Senator Mike Crapo. In his office I was able to attend congressional hearings, address, record and respond to constituent concerns, and provide private tours of the Capitol building to the Senator's guests. The senator allowed me to meet with several of his previous staff and colleagues to ask them questions about their career paths and to seek advice. I witnessed the President dedicate a new memorial and won the lottery to attend the lighting ceremony at the West Wing White House Lawn. I got to see diverse cultural norms and meet people from all over the world. I got to witness firsthand our nation's history and monuments. I am blessed beyond measure to have had the opportunity to work for the senator and live in the most powerful city in the world. That is where change happens, and it was surreal to be a part of the process.

My sister Amanda and I lost touch after our mother passed, and never fully reconnected. I held on to my feelings of anger, resentment, and bitterness against her. She heard that I was writing my story and asked if she could read it. I cautioned her that it was graphic, and that she would most likely be hurt by reading it. She insisted that she felt led to read it and proceeded. It's weird how life unfolds. Who would have thought that writing about what broke up my family would bring us back together? After reading to page seventeen, she was overcome with emotion. She took a short break, then went back and finished the story. She contacted me and asked if we could talk. I was reluctant, as I did not want to argue or bring up negative things from the past. I agreed to talk to her under certain conditions and set up boundaries to keep us both safe. I wanted to move at my own pace as she told me her side of the story. We cried on the phone for nearly three hours as she told me the same story through her eyes. My walls started coming down bit by bit as she filled in holes that my trauma-filled heart blocked out. She was compassionate and considerate as she answered questions I had previously been too fearful to ask. For the first time in a long while, I looked up to her. She made no excuses for being abusive but explained her reasoning. This is what she told me: "It took me years to understand why I did things the way I did. I will not make excuses, I know what I did was wrong. At least now I understand why, and can move forward. I became violent with you because it was how I became strong, being beaten. I wanted to make you strong, and that was the only way I knew how. I knew that you had to stand up for yourself, because no one would do it for you. I had to leave, and in doing so I was preparing you."

It doesn't completely make sense to me, but at least she realizes what she did and that it was wrong. It is a step in the right direction. As for me, I honestly can say that writing my story has helped me heal in countless ways. After talking to my sister, many memories that I shoved down back came up. Pieces of the puzzle are coming together, and it is starting to make sense. It has also started the process of restoring a relationship with my sister. While we will never be close, we have started the process of mending. Slowly and steadily, we are working on building trust again.

It is beautiful. Forgiveness is powerful.

When looking toward my future, I bear one thing in mind: my past has a purpose. It is not who I am, it is not how I define myself, but it is a part of me. I'm thankful for my past. It has made me appreciate life more, and has given me a reason to keep striving forward. I know I went through these things for a reason. I believe with all of my heart that it is because I now can help others in a way that only someone who has been there can. It is truly an honor to watch the system improving, and to be a part of that makes some of what I went through worth it. I will continue public speaking and hope that one day it will turn into a paid profession. I will keep loving, forgiving, and remembering. I will never forget where I have been, or where I want to go. I will be thankful for those that believed in me and encouraged me not to give up. And when the going gets rough, I will keep my eyes on the future, and the brightness of hope that brought me out of the darkness.

Author's note

When I started to write this book I hesitated for a few reasons. For one, I am not a professional writer; however, I am sure you are a forgiving crowd. I also feared being vulnerable and transparent; after all, this is my heart on paper. I did not want to be viewed as a victim, as I do not feel I am. It is difficult to share these experiences, and depending on my life at the time, some times are better than others. I still cry and experience anger and remorse; I am human. Perhaps my biggest fear was not being able to provide a happy ending to such a sad story.

The original copy of this book was published in 2011. It is now 2015, and I am revising it. I had wanted to revise the original now that I have grown, and more childhood memories have come back.

One day while driving I was thinking about my life, and where I was headed. I reminisced about speaking at a recent panel, and my heart fluttered as I saw people's hearts in the room change. A smile crossed my face as I recognized that I did have a happy ending.

I survived.

By no means am I saying that hope, courage, and small successes rid me of the scars and battles from my childhood. It is important to note that while I am emotionally mature and grounded, I am still affected daily by my upbringing. Thankfully, I have a surrogate family that encourages me, and sometimes they are my sanity. I suffer attachment and trust issues, but I am working on them. I now accept more of what happened, and let go of some of the baggage I was still lugging around. I am going through counseling through my church to deal with the grief associated with the trauma I experienced.

In November of 2013 I was saved. Since developing a relationship with Christ I have been able to grieve, honestly, for the first time. I have been able to be completely open and honest with myself, in dealing with my past. I don't have to be strong or hide my emotions. I am hurting deeper than ever before. Most of my life was compiled of struggle. I had learned to be a fighter. I survived, it's what I did. It was how I defined myself. Fighters do not have time to stop and grieve, because then they become vulnerable. I had no time for vulnerability. I had no time for second and third chances. I was not willing to be let down, or given up again. I was guarding my heart. I rationalized that if I didn't let anyone close, no one could hurt me. It has taken me years to understand why I think this way, and gradually I am getting better at allowing myself to be vulnerable and to trust. Through my faith I have been broken in myself, and am being built up in Him. It has changed the whole story for me. I am in no way pushing my faith on you, but that is what saved my soul. I think all of us need a savior, don't you?

A Special Note

Social Workers and Volunteer Child Advocates: I applaud you. It takes tremendous heart to endure what you do. I want to speak to you as a former foster youth. We may not be able to say it, but you are often our only advocate. Sometimes, you are the one consistent person in our lives. Know that expressing gratitude takes skills that most of our parents have not equipped us with. Know that each day, just by coming to work, you make a difference. I, personally, on behalf of all of the children you have helped, thank you. Thank you for stepping in where our parents failed, and for caring enough to sacrifice your own feelings to protect ours.

Current and Former Foster Youth: Hello brother/sister. I want you to know you're not alone. I hope that sharing my story has given you courage. I hope that I have shown you to not be ashamed of being a foster child, for that does not define YOU. All you have endured is for a reason. You have the power to make a difference! Remember, you are your own person. You are not limited, and you can do ANYTHING! Choose to be a warrior, not a victim of circumstance.

My future child: I love you already. I have spent my whole life preparing to love you the right way. When you read his I want you to know I waited for you. I waited until I could be the best parent possible. You are the greatest gift I could hope for, I hope you know that. I promise to always let you know how special you are, how valued and irreplaceable you are. I promise to let you see daily the place in my heart that only you can fill. I promise to allow you to have a childhood, and to prepare you for adulthood. I promise to be the best mother I can. And while I will never promise perfection, I promise to always strive in that direction.

To the reader: Thank you for opening your heart to hear my story, for listening, not judging, and seeking to find the good in this. If you are holding my book in your hand, you have contributed to my education. I thank you for your generosity. I hope that this book was worth your while, and somewhere along the way it touched you.

I would love to hear from you with any questions or feedback. I can be reached via e-mail at Kailalamai@gmail.com.

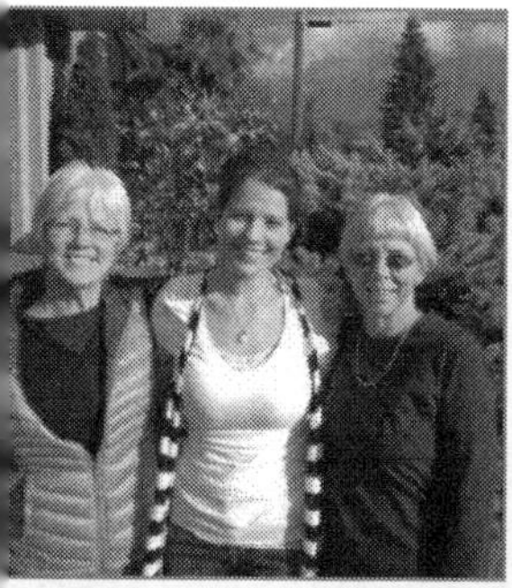
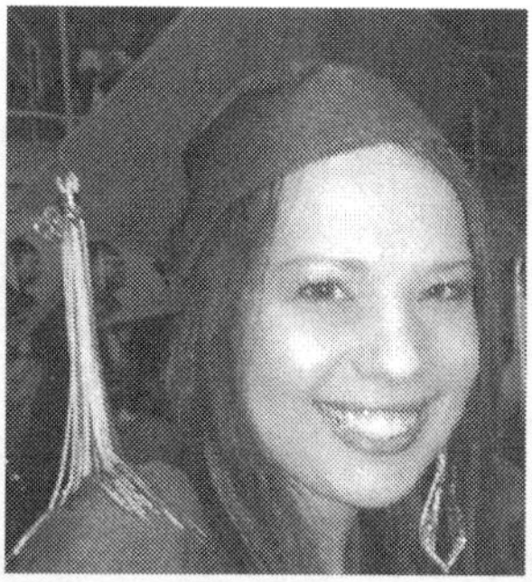
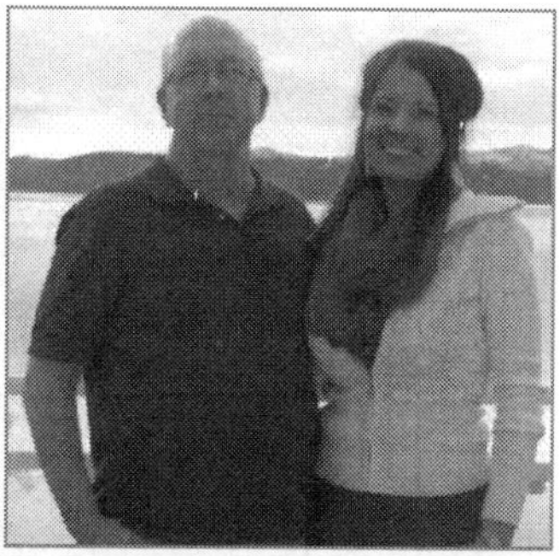
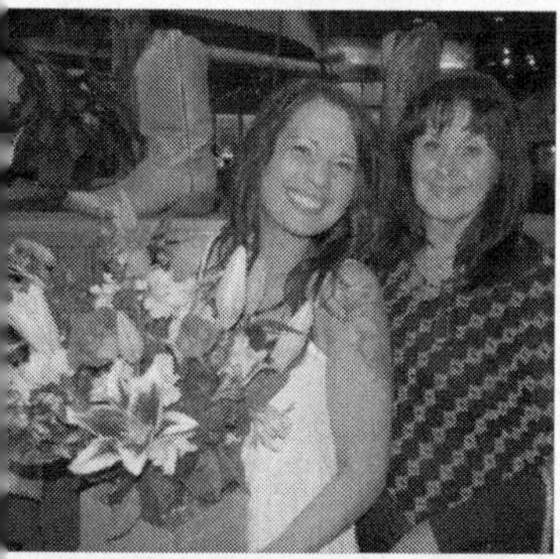
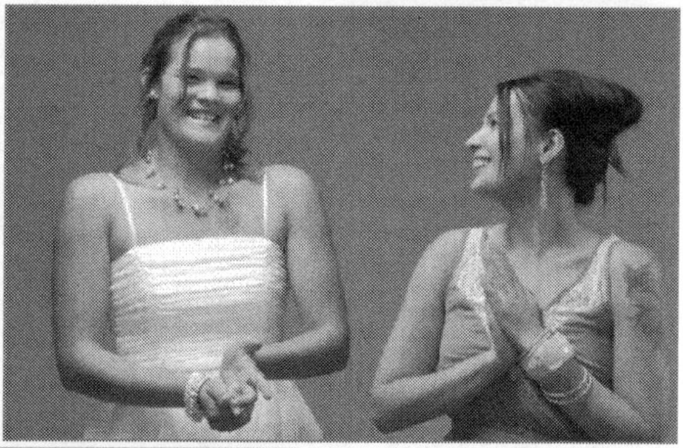
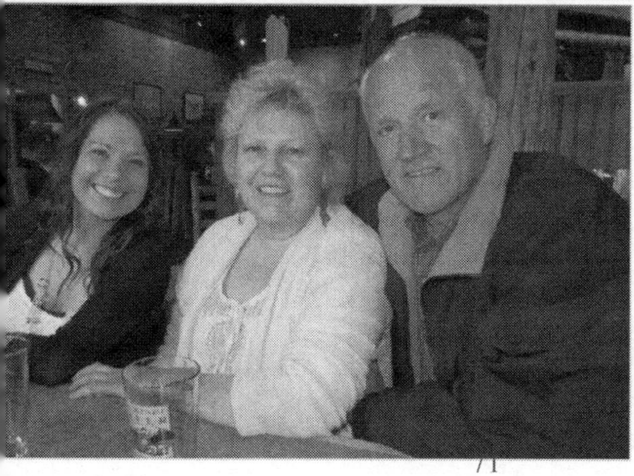
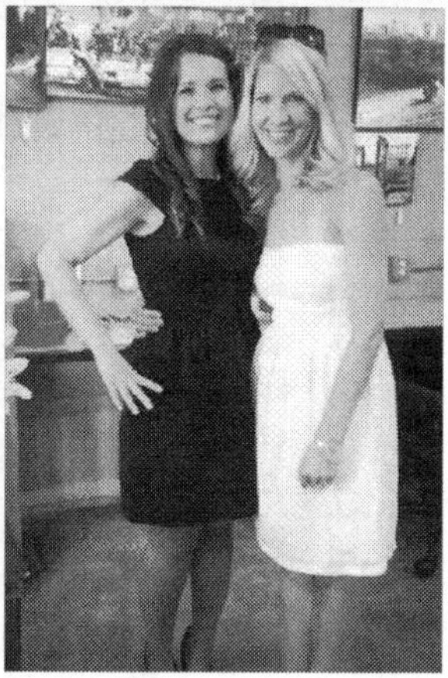

Resources that may be of help:

To apply for educational/living funding as a former foster child visit: http://www.fc2success.org/programs/education-training-vouchers/

To apply for federal aid for school visit: https://fafsa.ed.gov/

For healthy relationship information visit: http://kidshealth.org/teen/your_mind/relationships/healthy_relationship.html

To help Richard Paul Evans provide Lifestart kits to other children: http://www.thechristmasboxhouse.org/donate/

To become a CASA volunteer visit: http://www.casaforchildren.org/site/c.mtJSJ7MPIsE/b.5301309/k.9D58/Volunteering.htm

To report child abuse visit: https://www.childwelfare.gov/topics/responding/reporting

Made in the USA
San Bernardino, CA
18 April 2016